Inspired by and dedicated to
Abi & Zach

Copyright © Megan Knight 2021

All rights reserved.

No part of this publication may be reproduced, stored in a retrieval system, or transmitted, in any form, or by any means, electronic, mechanical, photocopying, recording or otherwise without the prior permission of the author.

ISBN: Paperback: 978-1-80227-050-1

eBook: 978-1-80227-051-8

MARVELLOUS MAGICAL CHAKRAS

Written & illustrated by
Megan Knight

Full of magical balls of light
MARVELLOUS CREATURES

We're marvellous, magical creatures,
Just look beyond the mirror.
Deep inside,
Where secrets lie.
You're a mythical being,
We'll not deny.

We're full of magical balls of light,
That spin around slowly out of sight.
Each one has a colour, a name, a job.
These mythical, magical, circular blobs.

It's time to come on a journey with me,
One where I can help you see.
Not with your eyes,
But with your heart.
So, if you're ready
It's time to start.

I know everything is connected
THE CROWN

Let's start from the top,
And work our way down.
All magical creatures deserve a crown.
Of course, this one shines nice and bright,
In violet, or purple, or sometimes white.

This mythical crown helps me to think,
I even wear it when I sleep.
It shows me things in my dreams,
And I think about what it means.

I have a crown,
And so do you.
So we have a connection,
That is true.

I use my eyes & inner voice to see
THE THIRD EYE

Magical creatures have magical eyes,
As a mythical, magical creature, so do I.
I've had one, and sometimes two,
but three's a charm, so that will do.

My third eye is indigo,
What an amazing colour!
But it can't be seen,
Not even by my brother.
It sits between my other two eyes,
And shows me things that try to hide.

The more I open it,
The more I see.
I'm pretty sure it talks to me.
It's like a little voice inside,
I have to say it's pretty wise.
When I listen carefully,
I can hear it guiding me.

I speak my truth
THE THROAT

Some creatures like to growl or screech,
Some have big mouths and scary teeth.
But I have a secret, as a mythical beast,
I actually use my throat to speak.

You might not believe it, but it's true,
And my throat is actually blue.
It helps me talk about how I feel,
Speak my truth,
And keep things real.

So, listen carefully when I speak,
The next time that we can get to meet.
I might say something you need to hear,
So, make sure that you use your ears.

I am loved and give love
THE HEART

Some creatures can give me the frights,
Especially if they visit at night.
Sometimes I hide underneath a chair,
And hope that they don't see me there.
But then I know I'll be OK,
I won't let these monsters stay in my way.

It's time to listen to my heart,
It's loving, it's kind, and it's pretty smart.
It sits in the centre of my chest,
 A sparkling gem beneath my vest.
You might see it in pink or green,
And it's definitely never, ever mean.

I love my monsters, I suddenly think.
No need to wash them down the sink.
I find the courage to give them a cuddle,
And watch them turn into beautiful bubbles.
 That I can gently blow away,
No longer afraid, I can shout Hooray!

I am confident in my power
THE SOLAR PLEXUS

Not too far below my heart,
Is a magical, yellow ball of art.
If you look closely you will see,
It has two strong arms,
This mystical, magical, part of me.

'I can', it shouts,
'I will', I say.
'Let's do this',
Then I go out and play.

It's full of little energy beans,
And confidence to just be me.
My little spinning Solar Plexus
Really is by far the bestest.

I feel happy and creative
THE SACRAL

So somewhere just below my navel,
Spins a super, orange Sacral.
This one gives me lots of pleasure,
Sensations, movement, it's hard to measure.

It likes to tell me how I feel,
I trust that what it says is real.
It helps me imagine exciting things,
Make new friends,
And share my dreams.

So, come along this ride with me,
And know you're where you're meant to be.

I am safe and grounded
THE ROOT

At the bottom of my spine,
Is a special place of mine.
Once in here, I know I'm safe.
I feel secure, inside this place.
I painted it my favourite colour,
A vibrant red, that's like no other.

Inside this very magical place
Suddenly I begin to change.
My toes spring into magical roots,
Thank goodness I'm not wearing boots!
Now I feel at one with nature,
I know that I am so much safer.

I call this home my Little Base,
I love this super amazing place.
It has a magical jar of money,
Protected by some mystical honey.
I know that I am where I belong,
In my root, my base, my special home.

Who am I again?
FEELING LOST

Some days are dark,
And my crown might slip.
My head is spinning in a mist.
And even though I'm sat at home,
I'm suddenly feeling all alone.

My third eye is tired,
And wants to close.
My throat is sore,
And wants to doze.
My heart feels broken, deep in two.
And now I'm feeling sad and blue.

My Solar Plexus has lost its shine,
So confidence is no longer mine.
My Sacral looks a different colour,
And took away my creative pleasure.
Now I'm no longer feeling safe,
Even in my Little Base.

But I can change this,
Trust in me.
Follow these steps, and I guarantee,
That I can pull you from the dark.
Let me show you where to start.

First, I get grounded
FINDING ME

Close your eyes,
And count to three.
Take a deep breath,
And imagine with me.
A bright white light comes down from the sky,
Are you beginning to wonder why?

The light is magical,
And here to help.
It casts a very special spell.
I see it moving through my body,
And now I feel a bit less foggy.

My roots spring out from the tips of my toes,
And now I know where they go.
Deep into the ground,
Holding me tight.
While I am full of a bright, white light.

A super clean
A HEALING LIGHT

As the bright light spins all around,
I see the purple of my crown.
Now it travels to my eye,
With magical rays of indigo sky.
Then I see my throat turn blue,
This light just knows what to do.

It carries onwards to my chest,
To visit my magical, sparkling gem.
Then my heart shines in brilliant green,
This light is doing a super clean.

Then I see it change to yellow,
Before it moves onto my sacral.
Finally, it reaches my little base,
Thank goodness I feel safe again.

I watch as all the colours spin,
Now I feel like a magical Queen.
I thank the light as it zoom's away,
There's just one more thing left to say.
I put myself in a golden bubble,
So I won't get into another muddle.

Happy being me
BRIGHT & BALANCED

And so, my friend,
We've reached the end.
I hope that you will come again.
Just remember what I advise,
It should be easy now you're wise.

If you ever do get into a muddle,
You might need more than just a cuddle.
Call upon your healing light,
Imagine it cleans your colours bright.

Put your roots into the ground,
And seal yourself all around.
I like to use a golden bubble,
I find it keeps me out of trouble.

We're all connected,
Never forget.
We're marvellous, magical, creatures,
With super, duper, hidden features.

www.ingramcontent.com/pod-product-compliance
Lightning Source LLC
Chambersburg PA
CBHW042235090526
44589CB00001B/10